Playing makes kids healthy and strong

$\mathcal{P}$laygrounds

Joanne Mattern

A⁺

Smart Apple Media

Smart apple 9/02 $14.95

COPYRIGHT

❖❖ Published by Smart Apple Media

1980 Lookout Drive, North Mankato, Minnesota 56003

Designed by Rita Marshall

Copyright © 2003 Smart Apple Media. International copyright reserved in

all countries. No part of this book may be reproduced in any form without

written permission from the publisher.

Printed in the United States of America

❖❖ Photographs by Dennis Frates, Herbert L. Gatewood, Gunter Marx

Photography, Tom & Sally Myers, Unicorn Stock Photos (Paula J. Harrington)

❖❖ Library of Congress Cataloging-in-Publication Data

Mattern, Joanne, 1963- Playgrounds / by Joanne Mattern. p. cm. — (Structures)

Includes bibliographical references and index.

Summary: Examines the history, equipment, and uses of playgrounds.

❖❖ ISBN 1-58340-148-2

1. Playgrounds—Juvenile literature. [1. Playgrounds.] I. Title. II. Structures

(North Mankato, Minn.)

GV423 .M37 2002   796'.06'8—dc21   2001049969

❖❖ First Edition 9 8 7 6 5 4 3 2 1

Playgrounds

CONTENTS

A Playful History

Children need play almost as much as they need food and shelter. But they did not always have safe, fun places to play. Before 1900, children played wherever they could find space. Children who lived in the country played in fields. City children played in the streets. ❖ Around 1900, a man in New York named Jacob Riis wrote newspaper articles. He said that playgrounds would help city children stay strong and healthy. Other people agreed with Riis. Soon, many cities began

A tire and a rope can turn a tree into a playground

building playgrounds for children. About the same time, playgrounds were also built in the country near schools. ❖

Early playground equipment was made of metal, and the ground under the equipment was covered with **asphalt**. Children were often hurt when they fell on the hard ground. The metal equipment was strong, but it was not safe. Children could be hit and injured by hard swings. Metal slides that sat in the sun often got hot enough to burn people! In 1945, Arnold White

Playground inspectors have an important job. They check playground equipment to make sure it is always safe to play on.

of Holliston, Massachusetts, created soft, flexible swing seats

from fabric belting. These were safer than wooden or metal

swings. ❖ People kept trying to make playgrounds safer.

The best playgrounds are safe playgrounds

Most playgrounds today are made of plastic

During the 1970s and 1980s, playgrounds were made of wood. But the wooden equipment sometimes **splintered** or cracked. Today, most new playground equipment is plastic. Plastic is strong and solid. It stays cooler in the hot sun. Best of all, it does not have sharp edges or rough surfaces that can hurt children.

From the Ground Up

Who decides what kind of playground to build? People who work at schools often plan playgrounds for the schoolyard. Playgrounds in parks are usually planned by a

council—a group of people who make important decisions—in

the town or village that owns the park. Sometimes, people in a

community decide they need a playground and build it

Playgrounds come in all shapes, even castles

GOWER WEST LEARNING CENTER
7650 Clarendon Hills Road
Willowbrook, IL 60514

themselves. ❖ To build a playground, people must first raise money. Then they decide what equipment they want to buy. That is the fun part! ❖ Once a community or school decides on the equipment, special playground **contractors** bring it to the site on big trucks. The contractors dig holes for the equipment and pour in concrete. The concrete hardens and holds the equipment in place.

The first playgrounds were covered with hard asphalt. Most playgrounds today are covered with pebbles, wood chips, or even soft rubber mats.

Types of Equipment

Today, playgrounds have a wide variety of equipment.

They have swings and slides. There are ladders, nets, jungle

Sometimes playgrounds are built by moms and dads

gyms, and monkey bars to climb. Some playgrounds have tunnels, sandboxes, or sprinklers. Because plastic is easy to **mold**, slides can be formed into unusual shapes. They may be wavy and feel like a bumpy road. Children get a dizzying ride on spiral and zigzag tube slides. ❖ Large playgrounds often have different equipment for younger and older children. Babies enjoy swings with high backs. Slides for young children are small

Some people work as playground leaders. Playground leaders plan games and other activities for children on playgrounds.

There are many kinds of playground equipment

and not very steep. Some playgrounds have picnic areas.

Others have basketball courts or baseball fields. Some even

have skating rinks and bike paths. Some playgrounds also have

swings that hold a wheelchair, or

climbing equipment with ramps and

handrails for children with disabilities.

Boston was the first American city to have play-grounds. In 1899, the city created sand lots where children could play.

❖ In Durnen, Holland, there is a

playground built for children of all ages. It is made of plastic

slides and tunnels. With slides sticking out of every side of a

central tower, the playground looks like a giant octopus!

Children at Play

For more than 100 years, children have gathered at playgrounds to make new friends and share activities.

This playground looks like a giant checkerboard

Playgrounds provide a safe, fun place where children can play.

That is important because, as Jacob Riis said so many years

ago, growing children need to play to stay healthy and strong.

When children play with others, they learn to take turns and

be friends. As they play on fun equipment, they can pretend

and let their imaginations soar. ❖ No matter if it is in the

country or the city, a playground will always be filled with the

same sounds—the shouts and laughter of children at play.

Playgrounds are good places to meet new friends

Slider Science

You can use a playground slide to conduct a scientific experiment.

What You Need

A slide
A marble
A piece of paper
A stopwatch or watch with a second hand

What You Do

1. Place the marble at the top of the slide. Use the watch to time how long it takes the marble to roll to the bottom.
2. Place the paper at the top of the slide and time how long it takes to reach the bottom.

What You See

The marble rolls down the slide faster than the piece of paper. The marble can move so quickly because it is round. Its round shape helps the surface of the marble keep moving over the slide. The paper moves slowly because its entire surface touches the slide at all times. This creates a lot of **friction** between the paper and the slide. This friction makes the paper move slowly.

The smoother a slide is, the faster it will be

INFORMATION

Index

Words to Know

asphalt (AZ-fawlt)—a black substance that is sticky when hot and hard when cool; it is used to make roads

community (kuh-MYOO-nuh-tee)—a group of people who live in the same area

contractors (KON-trak-torz)—people who build and install structures

friction (FRIK-shun)—the force that slows down objects when they rub against each other

mold (MOLD)—to bend or form into a certain shape

splintered (SPLIN-turd)—broken into sharp pieces

Read More

Boelts, Maribeth. *A Kid's Guide to Staying Safe at Playgrounds.* New York: PowerKids Press, 1997.

Dunn, Opal. *Acka Backa Boo: Playground Games from Around the World.* New York: Henry Holt & Co., 2000.

Gibbons, Gail. *Playgrounds.* New York: Holiday House, 1985.

Internet Sites

Games Kids Play
http://www.gameskidsplay.net

Hannah Williams Playground
http://www.hannahwilliams.org